G000256308

BRANCH LINES AROUND
1954 - 94
PORTHMADOG
The Welsh Highland and Festiniog Railways

Vic Mitchell and Keith Smith

 Middleton Press

Cover picture: To mark the 70th anniversary of the union of the FR and WHR, special trains were run for one weekend in June 1993. Coal- fired and recently restored, Palmerston waits to depart from Porthmadog for Minffordd at 14.50 on 5th June with nos. 39, 23 and 10 representing a typical WHR train of the 1920s. (V.Mitchell)

First published June 1994

ISBN 1 873793 31 6

© *Middleton Press 1994*

Design - Deborah Goodridge
Typesetting - Barbara Mitchell

Published by Middleton Press
　　　　Easebourne Lane
　　　　Midhurst
　　　　West Sussex
　　　　GU29 9AZ
　　　　Tel: (0730) 813169
(From 16 April 1995 - (01730) 813169)

Printed & bound by Biddles Ltd,
　　　　Guildford and Kings Lynn

INDEX

ACKNOWLEDGEMENTS

To those who have provided the photographs we express our deep gratitude, particularly to so many who have given much information and additional help at the same time. We are also grateful for the assistance given by J.Hewett (and indirectly others who have helped to compile the FR Chronology), G.Ive, Mr D. and Dr. S. Salter, M.Seymour (FR Company Archivist and producer of the diagrams in this album) and N.Stanyon.

Our sincere thanks for checking the manuscript for historical accuracy go to A.G.W. Garraway MBE, N.F.Gurley, A.Heywood, A.Ll.Lambert and M.Seymour.

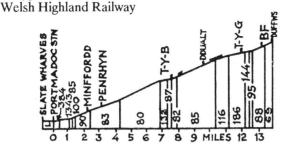

Simplified gradient profile of the FR in 1954

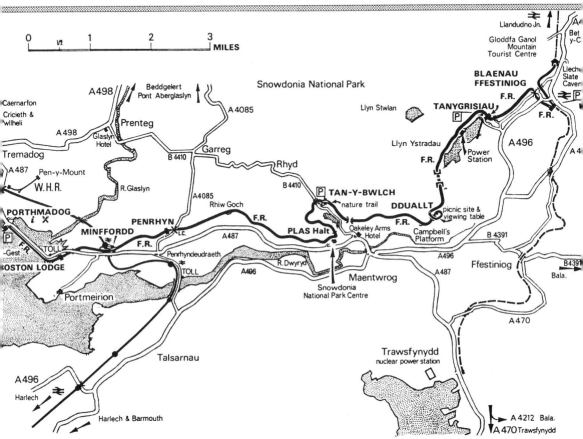

PLACE NAMES

During the nineteenth century great efforts were made by outsiders to anglicise Wales, resulting in confusion in the spelling of place names. For historical accuracy and consistency, the form used by the railways in the period covered by this book is generally adopted.

The Festiniog Railway's Act of Parliament was passed with only one "F" and so the railway's name cannot easily be changed, although it is now marketed with two.

In giving a guide to pronunciation, it must be assumed that the reader has heard the unique Welsh sound of "ll". The places are listed in journey order.

Portmadoc was renamed Porthmadog in 1974 despite having been built and named by Mr W.A.Madocks MP. The Welsh Prince Madog has gained fame for reputedly sailing to North America from a site north of the town, long before it existed. Both spellings are used in this album, depending on the period discussed.

Unfortunately, the three railways in Porthmadog are unhelpful to strangers by seldom making distinction between their stations, as was widely practised in the nineteenth century. Porthmadog North and Porthmadog Harbour would also be helpful to authors and their readers.

Minffordd	Mean-forth	Llyn Ystradau	*Ll*in erstradii
Penrhyn	Pen-reen	Tanygrisiau	Tan-er-grish-yah
Tan-y-bwlch	Tan-er-boolk	Blaenau	Bly-nigh
Dduallt	Thee-a*ll*t		

GEOGRAPHICAL SETTING

Portmadoc and its harbour were established in the 1820s, as the construction of the embankment or Cob resulted in the Afon Glaslyn scouring a deep channel near the tidal sluices. The port was suitable for the ships of the period and the town expanded as a result of the increasing trade, being laid out in a grid-iron pattern, as was common in new towns of industrial Britain.

The FR terminus is at the Harbour and its first mile traverses the level Cob. Thereafter the line was on a continuous rising gradient. To Penrhyndeudraeth the route is along a tapering finger of high ground that separates the valleys of the Glaslyn and the Dwyryd, the latter river being the main feature of the Vale of Ffestiniog. By Dduallt, the line is over 500ft above the valley floor and passes through part of the Moelwyn mountain range by means of a tunnel. In this vicinity granite was of economic importance, but the predominant mineral worked from here northwards is slate of high quality.

From Tanygrisiau the route runs up the valley of the Afon Barlwyd. It is in the urban area of Blaenau Ffestiniog for its final mile, being overshadowed by mountains and slate rubbish tips. The town is one of the highest in Wales at over 700ft above sea level.

The track diagrams herein are as in 1993.

KEY

FB	Foot-bridge
GS	Goods shed
LC(A)	Level crossing (automatic)
LC(G)	" " (gated)
GF	Ground frame
WT	Water tank
SB	Signal box

i Information
P Car park
▭ Inspection pit
—·— Fence
⋈ Gate

HISTORICAL BACKGROUND

Festiniog Railway

An Act of Parliament was obtained in 1832 for the construction of the line, which was intended to facilitate the conveyance of slates from the quarries of the Blaenau Ffestiniog district to the shipping wharves at the then new town of Portmadoc. Gravity and horses were to be the main sources of motive power on the route, which was (six years after opening) on a continuous down gradient to the sea and nearly 14 miles in length.

Traffic commenced in 1836 and increased greatly, necessitating the replacement of the horses by steam locomotives in 1863 for hauling the empty slate wagons back to the quarries. Passenger traffic started officially in 1865.

The line prospered as a general carrier, double engines being introduced in 1869 to increase capacity. Blaenau Ffestiniog was reached by the London & North Western Railway in 1879 and by the Great Western Railway in 1882. By the end of the century, these factors, combined with a decreasing demand for slate, resulted in substantially reduced revenue for the FR.

The demands of World War I reduced the maintenance of the line and its ability to meet the competition of the emerging road transport industry after 1918. Despite the development of tourism between the wars and the hopes of expanding this traffic in association with the 1923 Welsh Highland Railway, the company's fortunes continued to decline.

World War II resulted in the cessation of passenger services on 15th September 1939 but slate trains continued until 1st August 1946.

A number of people made abortive attempts to revive the decaying railway but it was the enterprise of a young man, Leonard Heath Humphrys who called a meeting in Bristol in 1951, which led to the formation of the Festiniog Railway Society. Mr Alan Pegler succeeded in gaining control of the historic company on 24th June 1954 when new directors were appointed and the controlling interest was passed to a trust. Mr. Allan Garraway became manager in June 1955 and general manager from 1958 to 1983. With the support of a small staff and many FRS members, passenger services were re-started from Portmadoc as follows:

To	Boston Lodge	23 July 1955
	Minffordd	19 May 1956
	Penrhyn	20 April 1957
	Tan-y-bwlch	5 April 1958
	Dduallt	6 April 1968
	Llyn Ystradau	25 June 1977
	Tanygrisiau	24 June 1978
	Blaenau Ffestiniog	25 May 1982

Some of the major events in the continuing development of this remarkable railway are illustrated in the following pages.

The prolonged legal battle to obtain compensation for the cost of reinstatement of the line submerged under a lake forming the lower part of a pumped storage hydro-electric system has been chronicled many times. Here we present pictures to indicate the magnitude of the task eventually undertaken to bypass the obstruction.

Welsh Highland Railway

Opening fully from Dinas Junction to Portmadoc on 8th June 1923, the WHR comprised three former concerns. From north to south, there was first the North Wales Narrow Gauge Railways which had been opened from Dinas Junction on the LNWR's 1872 Caernarvon-Afon Wen line. The NWNGR had begun passenger operation south to the west end of Quellyn Lake on 15th August 1877, being extended to the east end on 1st June 1878 and to Rhyd-Ddu (later South Snowdon) on 14th May 1881. Passenger services ceased on this line, and on its 1877 Bryngwyn branch, on 1st October 1916, the latter never to be restored. Goods traffic ran as required after 1916.

Secondly, under an Act of 1901, the Portmadoc, Beddgelert & South Snowdon Railway was incorporated, but the company achieved little, only the construction of a few earthworks and the ordering of *Russell* and six electric locomotives.

Thirdly, the horse-worked Croesor Railway had operated north-eastwards from Portmadoc since 1863/4, carrying slates from the quarries of the Croesor Valley to the harbour.

The WHR was formed in 1922 and was empowered under a Light Railway Order to complete the railway from South Snowdon to Portmadoc New, a new station south of the Cambrian Coast line, and it acquired the CR, NWNGR and the PB&SSR. ⟶

Passenger openings were thus:

31 July 1922   Dinas Jn. - South Snowdon
1 June 1923   South Snowdon-Portmadoc New
8 June 1923   Portmadoc New - Harbour

The line was a financial disaster, went into receivership in March 1927, was leased by the FR from 1st July 1934 and saw its last passenger train on 26th September 1936. An occasional goods train ran until 19th June 1937, closure following on 1st July 1937.

The decisions concerning the lease of the WHR were astonishing. A trial period from July to October 1934 was agreed for a nominal £1 rental but the WHR returned a hefty £506 loss during the first six months. Despite this, the FR committed itself to a 42-year lease. The terms were that 10% of gross receipts would be paid until 1948; an additional 5% on receipts over £2000pa was due until 1955 when the figures would be reviewed. In 1935 there was a loss of £496 to which £100 had to be added, representing the 10% of receipts. A similar loss was recorded for 1936, this being offset by the meagre profit made by operating the FR.

On the last day of 1936, the FR told the Investing Authorities that "both railways had been given equal publicity. Our experience, however, has been that the WHR does not appeal to the public in anything like the same degree as does our own railway. The latter has a length of 13 miles and travels an appreciable part of its line through scenery which is not open to the tourist by any other means of transport. In addition its known antiquity and recent centenary are other factors contributing in no small degree to its popularity. The WHR on the other hand, with its long length of 22 miles, though passing by or through such well known beauty spots as the Pass of Aberglaslyn and Beddgelert, has nothing but its novelty to recommend it to the public. The two places last mentioned are equally accessible by road". The FR sought to be released from the lease but this was refused. A further attempt succeeded in 1942, as there was by then no longer a railway that could be run. All steel had been removed under a Defence Regulations Requisition Order, lifting commencing in August 1941.

In 1961 a society was formed, which, three years later, was to become the Welsh Highland (1964) Ltd. Its objective was to reopen the whole of the line between Portmadoc and Dinas.

Several options were explored, using different sections of the WHR and also the former BR line to Caernarfon. Finally, in 1973 the Company took possession of the British Rail slate exchange siding in Portmadoc. This ran adjacent to the WHR project, intersecting it at Pen-y-Mount.

In 1978 Gelert's Farm was purchased, which lay in the triangle formed by the siding, the BR main line and the old WHR, so the company now had not only sufficient land on which to form a substantial base but also enough track to start their ambitious task, which would enable them to extend directly onto the old WHR trackbed.

Trains started to operate on 12th August 1980, carrying passengers on the one mile journey to the temporary terminus at Pen-y-Mount.

No less than five other bids for the trackbed have been made, including one from the FR. A Public Enquiry held in November 1993 should at last resolve the thorny problem of ownership. At the time of writing a decision is still awaited.

Considerable efforts have been made to revive the railway despite its inability to attract tourists in the 1930s. However its scenic attractions remain, but its long journey times cannot improve greatly.

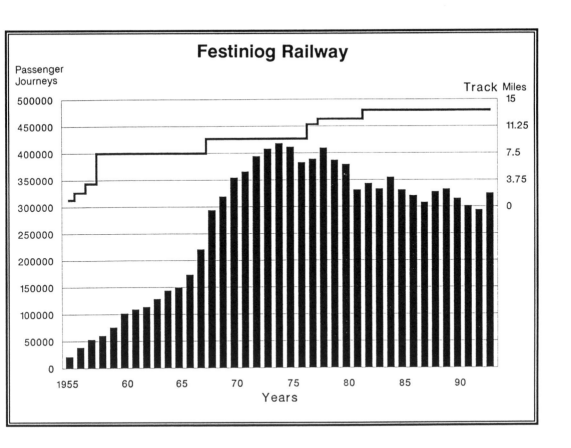

Festiniog Railway

Passenger
Journeys

Track Miles

1. The 1946 closure of the FR had been well documented in the railway press and so your author, Vic Mitchell, was amazed to find bright rails on his first visit to Blaenau Ffestiniog on 21st June 1951. They are seen at the former GWR platform, their brightness being due to their use by slate trains between the Maenofferen Quarry incline and the former LMSR and GWR exchange sidings. The diesel locomotive used for this traffic (which continued until 1962) was kept in a shed under Queen's Road bridge (left). Thus it can be claimed that at least some part of the FR has been in use since 1836. On the right, an ex-GWR 0-6-0PT stands at the head of a train from Bala. (V.Mitchell)

FESTINIOG RAILWAY COMPANY

TRAIN SERVICE

PORTMADOC (Harbour) and BOSTON LODGE (for Port Meirion). 1955

PORTMADOC Dep.

10.30, 11.30 a.m., 1.30 (x), 2.30, 3.30, 4.30, 5.30 p.m.

BOSTON LODGE Dep.

11.00 a.m., 12 noon, 3.00, 4.00, 5.00, 6.00 p.m.

X. Runs when required.

FARE 1/- Return. 8d. Single.

(CHILDREN UNDER 14 HALF PRICE).

The Festiniog Railway was the prototype of narrow gauge railways throughout the world. It was opened in 1836, and steam traction was introduced in 1863, with the locomotives "PRINCE" and "PRINCESS." The passenger Service was suspended in 1939 and the line closed in 1946.

The control of the shares of the Company was obtained by a railway enthusiast in 1954, and a new Board of Directors formed. Railway enthusiasts are supporting the Railway Company financially through the Festiniog Railway Society, and nearly all the work done in restoring the line has been done by voluntary effort. Your patronage and support will aid the railway to reopen further stretches through glorious scenery, in following years.

The original locomotive "PRINCE" has been reconditioned and is once more hauling trains.

A. G. W. GARRAWAY, Manager.

FESTINIOG RAILWAY COMPANY

1956

TIME TABLE

SATURDAY, 19th MAY TO SATURDAY, 22nd SEPTEMBER INCLUSIVE, WEEK-DAYS ONLY
ALSO SUNDAY, 20th MAY AND SUNDAY, 5th AUGUST

UP TRAINS

	X	X				
Portmadoc	11.00	12.00	2.00	3.00	4.00	5.00
Pen Cob Halt	A	A	A	A	A	A
Boston Lodge	11.07	11.07	2.07	3.07	4.07	5.07
Minffordd	11.14	12.14	2.14	3.14	4.14	5.14

DOWN TRAINS

	X	X				
Minffordd	11.30	12.30	2.30	3.30	4.35	5.30
Boston Lodge	11.37	12.37	2.37	3.37	4.42	5.37
Pen Cob Halt	A	A	A	A	A	A
Portmadoc	11.44	12.44	2.44	3.44	4.49	5.44

NOTES

A. Passengers wishing to alight at Pen Cob Halt (for the Beach) must advise the guard at Minffordd or Portmadoc. Passengers wishing to join the train must signal the driver to stop.

X Runs 16th July to 8th September only, NOT Sunday, August 5th.

Special trains for parties at other times by prior arrangement.

All enquiries should be addressed to :—

THE MANAGER,
FESTINIOG RAILWAY COMPANY,
PORTMADOC,
CAERNS.

A. G. W. GARRAWAY, *Manager.*

T. STEPHENSON & SONS LTD., PRINTERS, PRESCOT, LANCS.

FESTINIOG RAILWAY COMPANY

1957

TIME TABLE

WEEK DAYS, 5th JUNE—28th SEPTEMBER.
ALSO WHIT SUNDAY AND AUGUST SUNDAY

UP TRAINS

	A	A					B
Portmadoc	11.00	12.00	2.00	3.00	4.00	5.00	7.30
Minffordd	11.12	12.12	2.12	3.12	4.12	5.12	7.42
Penrhyndeudraeth	11.20	12.20	2.20	3.20	4.20	5.20	7.50
Tan-y-Bwlch	Service temporarily suspended						
Dduallt							
Tan-y-Grisiau							
Blaenau Ffestiniog							

DOWN TRAINS

	A	A					B
Blaenau Ffestiniog	Service temporarily suspended						
Tan-y-Grisiau							
Dduallt							
Tan-y-Bwlch							
Penrhyndeudraeth	11.30	12.30	2.30	3.30	4.30	5.30	8.00
Minffordd	11.38	12.38	2.38	3.38	4.38	5.38	8.08
Portmadoc	11.50	12.50	2.50	3.50	4.50	5.50	8.20

A. Week-days only, 15th July—7th September, also Whit Monday.
B. Tuesdays, Wednesdays, Thursdays, and Saturdays, 16th July—7th September. Also Whit Saturday and Whit Monday.
All trains call at Pen Cob, Boston Lodge and Pen-y-Bryn halts by request.
All enquiries should be addressed to :—
The Manager, Festiniog Railway Company, Portmadoc, Caerns.
Tel. Portmadoc 2340

A. G. W. GARRAWAY, *Manager*

FESTINIOG RAILWAY COMPANY

TIME TABLE - 1958

WEEKDAYS ONLY, 24th MAY-27th SEPTEMBER, also 5th and 7th APRIL
SUNDAYS, 6th APRIL, 25th MAY and 3rd AUGUST
WEDNESDAYS ONLY, 9th APRIL-21st MAY and 1st-22nd OCTOBER —(See Note A)

(Photo by courtesy of the English Electric Co. Ltd.)

	PWLLHELI	dep.	9S25	9E55	12.45			
	PORTMADOC (W)	arr.	9S56	10E23	1.14			
	BARMOUTH	dep.		9.25	12.20	2S40	3E45	
	MINFFORDD	arr.		10.15	1.12	3S21dd	4E36	
	PORTMADOC (W)	arr.			1.16	3S26		
				B				C
0	PORTMADOC (Harbour)	dep.		10.40	2.30		4.30	7.30
¼	PEN COB (Halt)	,,		dd	dd		dd	....
1	BOSTON LODGE (Halt)	,,		dd	dd		dd	dd
2¼	MINFFORDD (for B.R. (W))	,,		10.52	2.42		4.42	dd
3	PEN-Y-BRYN (Halt)	,,		dd	dd		dd	....
3¼	PENRHYN	,,		10.58	2.48		4.48	dd
7¼	TAN-Y-BWLCH	arr.		11.25	3.15		5.15	8.10
9	DDUALLT	Service temporarily suspended						
12	TAN-Y-GRISIAU							
13¼	BLAENAU FFESTINIOG							
0	BLAENAU FFESTINIOG	Service temporarily suspended						
1¼	TAN-Y-GRISIAU							
4¼	DDUALLT			B				C
5¼	TAN-Y-BWLCH	dep.		11.45	3.30		5.30	8.40
10	PENRHYN	,,		12.12	3.57		5.57	dd
10¼	PEN-Y-BRYN (Halt)	,,		dd	dd		dd	....
11	MINFFORDD (for B.R. (W))	,,		12.18	4.03		6.03	dd
12¼	BOSTON LODGE (Halt)	,,		dd	dd		dd	dd
12¼	PEN COB (Halt)	,,		dd	dd		dd	....
13¼	PORTMADOC (Harbour)	arr.		12.30	4.15		6.15	9.20
	PORTMADOC (W)	dep.		1.17	4.35			
	MINFFORDD	dep.		1.22	4.40		6.08	
	BARMOUTH	arr.		2.12	5.27		6.57	
	MINFFORDD	dep.			4E31		6.17	
	PORTMADOC (W)	dep.		1.20	4E48	4S32	6.20	
	PWLLHELI	arr.		1.55	5E20	5S05	7.00	

Western Region times shown apply 9th June-13th September, week-days only.
A. On Wednesdays only, 9th April-21st May and 1st-22nd October, the 3-30 train will leave Tan-y-Bwich at 3.45 and run 15 minutes later throughout. The 4.30 from Portmadoc and 5-30 from Tan-y-Bwich will not run.
B. Runs 30th June-13th September, week-days only, also Easter Monday, 7th April.
C. Runs Tuesday, Wednesday, Thursday and Saturday only, 8th July-4th September, also Whit Saturday and Monday, May 24th and 26th.
Trains marked B and C may also run on other days by prior arrangement.
E. Except Saturdays. S. Saturdays only.
dd Calls when required to set down on notice to the Guard at previous stopping station; passengers wishing to join should give the necessary hand signal to the Driver.

PASSENGER SERVICES

The company's timetables for the first four years of revival are reproduced on the left. They became progressively more complex in terms of seasonal and daily variations and so on this page we show only the Monday-Friday service for the peak traffic periods for the years of the reopening of fresh lengths of line. The extracts are reproduced from BR timetables.

Only in 1957 did the FR serve local needs to any extent, the fairly frequent service to Penrhyn being of value to the residents of the upper part of that place. The winter timetable is shown near picture no. 61.

1968	21 July to 1 September **Mondays to Fridays**												FX	FX
PORTMADOC d	10 00	10 40	11 30	12 25	13 20	14 15	15 05	16 00	16 50	17 45	19 45		
BOSTON LODGE.. d	b	b	b	b	b	b	b	b	b	b	b		
MINFFORDD . a	10 09	10 49	11 39	12 34	13 29	14 24	15 14	16 09	16 59	17 54	19 54		
d	10 10	10 50	11 42	12 37	13 31	14 26	15 19	16 11	17 03	17 56	19 56		
PENRHYN .. d	b	b	b	b	b	b	b	b	b	b	b		
TAN-Y-BWLCH .. a	10 35	11 15	12 07	13 02	13 56	14 51	15 44	16 36	17 28	18 21	20 21		
d	10 40	11 20	12 12	13 07	14 01	14 56	15 48	16 41	17 33	18 26	20 26		
DDUALLT ... a	10 50	11 30	12 22	13 17	14 11	15 06	15 58	16 51	17 43	18 36	20 36		

b Stops when required to set down on notice to the Guard. Passengers wishing to join the train must give a hand signal to the Driver.

FX Fridays excepted

1977 — Daily Saturday 21 May to Sunday 25 September

	A	A	B	A	A	B	A	A	B	C	D
		[3]			[3]			[3]			
Porthmadog .. .. d	09 45	10 15	10 45	11 15	12 15	12 45	13 15	13 45	14 45	15 15	15 45	16 15	17 15	19 15
Boston Lodge.................... d	x		x		x		x		x		x		x	x
Minffordd .. .. d	09 55	10 25	10 55	11 25	12 25	12 55	13 25	13 55	14 55	15 25	15 55	16 25	17 25	19 25
Penrhyn .... d	10 03	10 33	11 03	11 33	12 33	13 03	13 33	14 03	15 03	15 33	16 03	16 33	17 33	19 33
Tan-y-Bwlch .... d	10 25	10 55	11 25	11 55	12 55	13 25	13 55	14 25	15 25	15 55	16 25	16 55	17 55	19 55
Blaenau Ffestiniog 🚌 .... a						14 00*				16 41				
Dduallt .... d	10 40	11 10	11 40	12 10	13 10	13 40	14 10	14 40	15 40	16 10	16 40	17 10		20 10
Llyn Ystradau.................... a	10 50	11 20	11 50	12 20	13 20	13 50	14 20	14 50	15 50	16 20	16 50	17 20		20 20
Tan y Grisiau														
Blaenau Ffestiniog..................														

A Mondays to Fridays 11 July to 2 September also Spring Holiday week 6 to 10 June and Sundays 5 June and 28 August

B Mondays to Fridays 23 May to 23 September also Saturdays and Sundays 4, 5 June and 9 July to 28 August

C Mondays to Thursdays 6 to 9 June and 11 July to 1 September, Sundays 5 June and 28 August

D Mondays to Thursdays 6 to 9 June and 11 July to 1 September, Wednesdays 25 May to 6 July and 7 to 21 September, Saturdays 4 June and 9 July to 27 August, Sundays 22 May to 18 September

🚌 Connection by bus between Tan-y-Bwlch station and Blaenau Ffestiniog (Monday to Friday only 23 May to 23 September)

• Mondays to Fridays. To Llechwedd Caverns arrive 5 minutes later .

1978 — Mondays to Fridays 22 May to 22 September

Miles		A	A	A	A	G FX		A	H	B FX
0	Porthmadog .. .. .. d	09 30	10 00	11 00	11 30	..	12 00	12 30	13 30	..	14 00	14 30	15 00	..	16 00	16 30	19 00	..
—	Pwllheli..................75 d	07 57	07 57	10 34	10 34	....		12 14		12 14				....	14 55		17 20	..
—	Barmouth .. .. .. 75 d	08 17	08 17	10 05	10 05	....			13 26					....		15 27	17 37	..
2	Minffordd.................... d	09 40	10 10	11 10	11 40	..	12 10	12 40	13 40	..	14 10	14 40	15 10	..	16 10	16 40	19 10	..
3½	Penrhyn .. .. d	09 45	10 15	11 15	11 45	..	12 15	12 45	13 45	..	14 15	14 45	15 15	..	16 15	16 45	19 15	..
7½	Tan-y-Bwlch .... d	10 10	10 40	11 40	12 10	..	12 40	13 10	14 10	..	14 40	15 10	15 40	..	16 40	17 10	19 40	..
12½	Tan-y-Grisiau .. .. .. a	10 36	11 06	12 06	12 36	..	13 06	13 36	14 36	..	15 06	15 36	16 06	..	17 06	17 36	20 06	..
13½	Blaenau Ffestiniog 🚌 ...... a		11 52	12 23	13 22	..		14 22		..	15 22		16 22	..		17 47		..
	Llandudno Junction .. .. 84 a	..	13 29	13 29	15c07	..	....		....	..	....		17 24	..	..	18c49		..

A 29 May to 2 June, also 10 July to 1 September

B Mondays to Thursdays 29 May to 1 June and 10 July to 31 August, also Wednesdays 24 May, 7 June to 5 July and 6, 13, 20 September

G 29 May to 1 June also 10 July to 31 August

H Not Fridays 2 June and 14 July to 1 September

1982 — Mondays to Fridays 31 May to 29 October

	A FX	B	B	B	B	A FX	B	A FX
Porthmadog Harbour .. .. d	08 45	09 55	10 40	11 30	12 25	13 15	14 05	15 00	15 50	16 40	19 00
Minffordd .... d	08 54	10 04	10 49	11 39	12 34	13 24	14 15	15 09	15 59	16 49	19 09
Penrhyn .... d	Early Bird	10 10	10 55	11 45	12 40	13 30	14 20	15 15	16 05	16 55	19 15
Tan-y-Bwlch.................... d		10 30	11 18	12 10	13 00	13 50	14 40	15 35	16 25	17 15	19 35
Tanygrisiau .. .. .. d		10 50	11 40	12 30	13 20	14 10	15 04	15 55	16 48	17 35	19 55
Blaenau Ffestiniog................ a	09 45	11 00	11 50	12 38	13 30	14 22	15 12	16 05	16 56	17 45	20 10

Most trains stop at Boston Lodge, Plas Halt, Campbell's Platform and Dduallt on request

WELSH HIGHLAND
RAILWAY

2. The Porthmadog terminus is close to the BR station (behind the camera), their Cambrian Coast line being evident on the right. Bagnall 0-4-2T *Gelert* is nearing the end of its run on 12th July 1993 and is approaching the station, which includes a buffet and a good railway bookshop. (D.W.Allan)

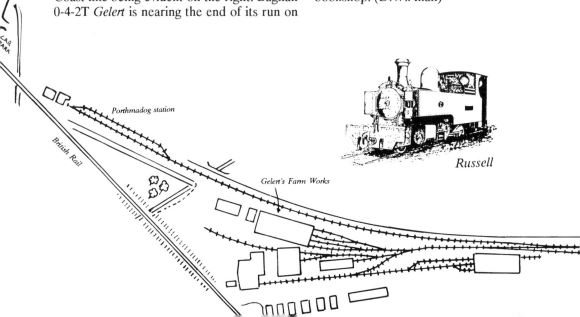

Russell

3. Porthmadog is largely obscured by Gelert's Farm Works, the company's centre for restoration and maintenance of its fleet of unusual rolling stock. Curving past on the right is the WHR main line, which was laid on the site of the GWR siding shown in pictures 42 and 43 in *Branch Lines around Portmadoc 1923-46*. (D.W.Allan)

4. The northern limit of operation is Pen-y-Mount, where a loop and engineers siding is provided. The original route of the WHR (behind the railings) once continued into the town, passing close to the tall mill building seen left of centre in this 1993 view. (D.W.Allan)

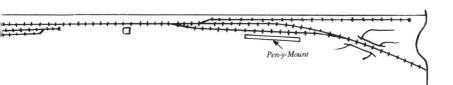

Pen-y-Mount

5. The ex-World War I Simplex performed one of the first shunting movements at Harbour station since its closure, to the delight of the local youth who arrived like wasps to a jam pot. This is the scene on 2nd October 1954 when the boiler and power bogie of 0-6-4T *Moel Tryfan* were positioned ready for the scrap merchant's cutting torch. The manager later regretted this move although it seemed appropriate then, owing to the desperate need for cash. Much stock had been abandoned at the station after the cessation of passenger services in 1939, as what little traffic there was thereafter was destined for the wharves. (A.G.W.Garraway)

6. Prior to reopening on 23rd July 1955, this test train was run on 20th. It comprises coaches nos. 23 and 12 hauled by the then petrol-engined Simplex, devoid of armour plating at one end to improve air flow to the radiator. It worked all trains until 2nd August and was officially named *Mary Ann* in 1971. (A.G.W.Garraway)

7. Only minor track repairs had been undertaken by the time that this selection of rolling stock was assembled for the FRS AGM on 24th March 1956. The lifeless and unrestored *Merddin Emrys* stands with nos. 15, 17, 22, 23 and 12. Also included are the General Manager's MG and the company's hearse (left). A special train ran from Paddington in 1957 in connection with the AGM. (A.G.W.Garraway)

8. *Prince* hauled the last train across Britannia Bridge on 2nd September 1958, the wharves on the left having long been abandoned. The gateposts behind the tender still carried the marks from passing slate wagons in 1993 although the site is occupied by the Community Centre. (A.G.W.Garraway)

9. The track in this and the previous picture was laid in 1923 to connect the FR with the WHR (*see Branch Lines around Portmadoc 1923-46* pics. 56-60). The rails were lifted from the bridge in 1958 but those at the south end of Madoc Street remained until 18th March 1960. A petrol station now occupies the site on the right. (A.G.W.Garraway)

10. Seen from the upper floor of Harbour station, South Snowdon Wharf provided an ideal location for BBC TV to relay signals from a train (aerials in the foreground) to the top of Snowdon, from where a fixed link was used. Here we see trials in progress on 15th April 1959 in readiness for a live broadcast on 13th July 1960. At this time, part of the former wharf siding was used for loco coal wagons. (A.G.W.Garraway)

11. The unusual stub points were removed on 1st March 1964 and put to use in the sidings of Glan-y-Mor yard, beside Boston Lodge Works. They were later moved to Minffordd Yard. On the left is coach no. 11, converted to an observation car in 1958. It was the first such bogie vehicle on the railway and the only one until 1965. (N.F.Gurley)

12. An eastward view in the mid-1960s presents a tranquil scene with the station buildings reflected in the still waters of the harbour, few cars in sight and the high-density housing yet to come. Minffordd is close to the nearest of the then new pylons. (N.F.Gurley)

13. The level crossing and coal stage seen in the previous picture disappeared when this new track was laid in 1964. Coal is stacked near the water tower. The wall on the right is on the left of the last view. (N.F.Gurley)

14. Standing on the former connection to the Welsh Highland Railway (see *Branch Lines around Portmadoc 1923-46* pic.65) on 23rd March 1966 is the world's first Beyer-Garratt locomotive. This class K 0-4-4-0T spent its working life in Tasmania, returned to its birthplace in Manchester and was purchased by the FR for £1000. Too large to work on the line, it was sent to York on 25th June 1976, on long-term loan as a museum exhibit. (N.F.Gurley)

15. The coal siding on the left was slightly elevated to reduce the height that the fuel had to be lifted to the stage, which was almost level with the locomotive bunkers. On the right is the new road to serve the controversial housing development which has ruined the view for ever. *Taliesin* was renamed *Earl of Merioneth* in 1961, withdrawn in 1971 and sent to York Railway Museum in 1988, bearing its original name *Livingston Thompson*. (N.F.Gurley)

17. By 1971 a clock graced the goods shed wall, while television aerials had come to adorn Britannia Terrace. Next to no. 11 is no. 12, the FR's first buffet car, so equipped in 1957. They had both been built as bogie brake vans in 1880 and were partially fitted with passenger accommodation in the late 1920s. (Festiniog Railway Co.)

16. Most of the platform had a loose surface with slate slab edging when photographed on 1st November 1970. *Mountaineer* (right) waits to depart at 13.20 with a special, while *Merddin Emrys* stands with the stock of the 14.30 departure. Moving with the times, the FR had adopted the 24-hour clock. (A.N.Massau)

18. Track work is delayed as ex-Penrhyn Railway *Linda* shunts a van in August 1974. Sister engine *Blanche* is on the left. Many of the historic four-wheeled coaches standing in front of the goods shed were used to strengthen trains at times of peak demand. Britannia Foundry (right) supplied the FR with firebars for many years until closure in 1965. (P.Barnfield)

19. Lack of sufficient space for the shop, buffet, museum and offices resulted in this extension in 1974. The former goods shed (right) has served variously to house the manager's car, rolling stock and a local contractor working on carriage rebuilding. Later it became the museum. (N.F.Gurley)

20. Seen in June 1975, the new ground-floor window served the "Little Wonder" buffet, a name also used on the first double engine in 1869. On the left are the original booking hall doors. Until 1960 there was no direct access to the hall from the car park, formerly a slate wharf. (N.F.Gurley)

21. On 24th June 1978, the first passenger service through to Tanygrisiau since 1939 commenced. *Blanche* (right) departed at 11.00 with ten coaches loaded with "Deviationists" (those involved in the construction of the new deviation route - see pictures 80 to 97). *Merddin Emrys*, carrying the headboard, hauled the train conveying invited guests, together with FR and FRS officials, 30 minutes later. The first public train was at 15.00. (N.F.Gurley)

22. The FR excels at obtaining publicity (and usually revenue) from special events. On the occasion of *Princess* retiring to the museum on 22nd April 1981, a special display of locomotives was arranged. From left to right - *Blanche, Prince,* the 1979 *Earl of Merioneth* and *Merddin Emrys.* (N.F.Gurley)

23. The coal stage was removed in March 1973, with the introduction of oil firing, and this water tank was erected in the following May. Nearest is coach no. 111, built in 1990 and fitted with a driving compartment for push-pull working with diesel locomotives. A platform canopy was donated in 1965, it having adorned the Town Hall until that time. It was not possible to erect then and passengers had to wait until 1987 for this new fabricated structure to protect them from inclement weather. (N.F.Gurley)

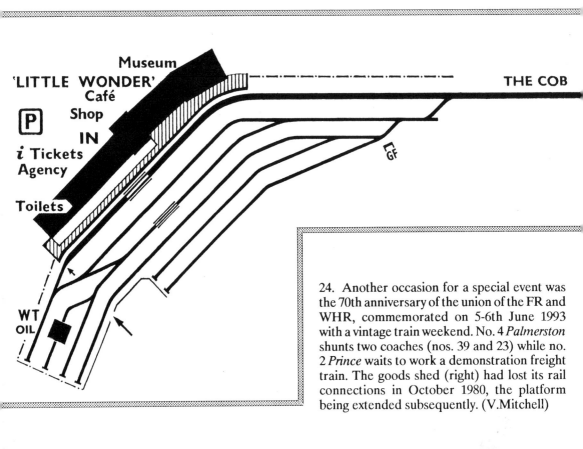

Museum

'LITTLE WONDER'

Café

Shop

THE COB

P

IN

i Tickets
Agency

GF

Toilets

WT
OIL

24. Another occasion for a special event was the 70th anniversary of the union of the FR and WHR, commemorated on 5-6th June 1993 with a vintage train weekend. No. 4 *Palmerston* shunts two coaches (nos. 39 and 23) while no. 2 *Prince* waits to work a demonstration freight train. The goods shed (right) had lost its rail connections in October 1980, the platform being extended subsequently. (V.Mitchell)

BOSTON LODGE

25. This photograph records the first locomotive movement on the FR south of Blaenau Ffestiniog for over eight years. The Simplex was coaxed back to life on the morning of 21st September 1954 and was driven to the yard gates where deep wind-blown sand prevented further progress. Coaches 10 and 17 were hauled to Harbour Station two days later. (A.G.W.Garraway)

26. By January 1955 the yard had been partially cleared; this view including the ends of the hearse, no. 1 and no. 3. The foundry chimney was a reminder that the works had once been capable of providing everything that the railway neded and was an example for others to emulate. Apathy in 1946 meant that coal was left in the bunkers of the locomotives, which were abandoned ungreased.
(A.G.W.Garraway)

27. A photograph from the Spring of 1955 reveals that some "new" sleepers had arrived, paid for by the sale of scrap metal. The other remains of *Moel Tryfan* in the foreground were soon to go in that cause. The six-wheeled wagon has a flexible wheelbase on the Cleminson principle (see our *Branch Line to Southwold*) and had been used from the 1920s for the carriage of flour. Its roof was soon removed so that it could carry loco coal. An appeal for funds for its restoration was started in 1993.
(R.D.Smith)

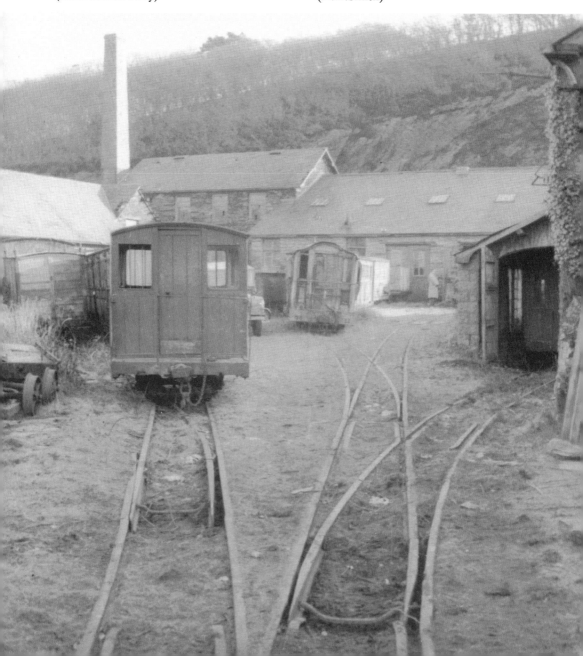

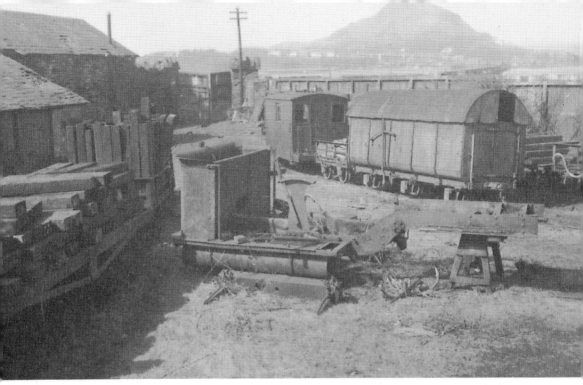

28. This April 1955 picture of the former locomotive shed should be compared with nos. 79 and 80 in *Branch Lines around Portmadoc 1923-46*. After roof repairs it was used as a carriage shed but the locomotive water supply (tanks on the extreme right) was beyond recommissioning. A small tank was placed on top of the gate pillar above the toll-house for the 1955 services. (A.G.W.Garraway)

29. The toll-house is the white-walled building and the white-roofed shed on the left was seen in the previous picture. The quarry on the right provided the rock for the construction of The Cob (the embankment across the estuary). Extreme right in this May 1956 view are the former gunpowder stores (magazines) from which explosive was carried up the line to the quarries. (A.G.W.Garraway)

30. Nos. 11 and 12 follow *Taliesin* round the curve shortly before the iron fence to the works yard was removed in August 1958 to give passengers a view of other locomotives. A Bond three-wheeler is parked by the bridge which once spanned an inclined road into the yard. (N.F.Gurley)

31. A line of coal wagons stands in the works yard in November 1958, while coaches stand in Glan-y-Mor yard awaiting restoration. The nearest one is on the site of a carriage shed which collapsed onto stored coaches, necessitating its demolition in 1956. (A.G.W.Garraway)

32. Another 1958 photograph shows *Taliesin* together with the massive gate pillars which are in line with those of the toll gate. Motor traffic was so light in those days that only one gate was usually open. By then the timber store was devoid of slates prior to its demolition in 1962. (N.F.Gurley)

33. On the right is the framework of the new carriage shed which was erected as an exercise by Royal Engineers in March 1964. Clearance for new sidings is in progress, the nearest containing the "white" figure of *Palmerston*, its last coat of paint having been part of some merriment in connection with ghosts. (N.F.Gurley)

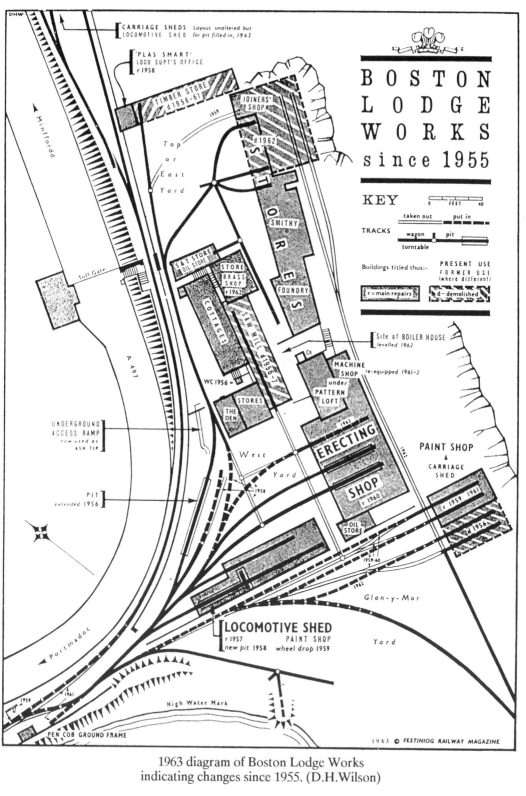

1963 diagram of Boston Lodge Works
indicating changes since 1955. (D.H.Wilson)

34. The framing had to wait until August 1967 before cladding could be applied, owing to budget limitations. The adjacent yard was the depository for permanent way materials, Minffordd eventually becoming the hub of this activity. (N.F.Gurley)

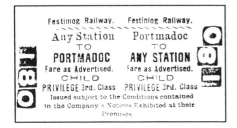

35. A 1971 view shows *Blanche* receiving oil from a tank wagon, *Linda* having been the first FR locomotive to be converted to oil firing in April of that year. The device to the left of the locomotive servicing pit is a sand drier. (Festiniog Railway Co.)

36. This photograph was taken from the top of the foundry chimney seen in pictures 26 and 35, just prior to its demolition in November 1978 due to its unsafe condition. *Moel Hebog* is in the centre and oil tanks abound. For many years the bogie wagon worked on Nocton Estates, carrying potatoes prior to their conversion to Smiths Crisps. (N.F.Gurley)

37. The Glan-y-Mor carriage shed and associ-
ated workshops were well advanced when recorded on 15th August 1979, much volunteer
labour having been used on the project. *Pal-*
merston and the ex-Harrogate Gasworks Pec-
kett 0-6-0ST are in the foreground while the
background includes the stub points seen in
picture no. 11. (N.F.Gurley)

38. On 22nd April 1981 all the operational locomotives ran to Harbour station when *Princess* entered the museum, as recorded in picture no. 22. In the works gateway is *Mountaineer*, followed by *Princess, Prince* and *Diana*. In the background is Pen Cob ground frame shelter. A halt was in use here from May 1956 until November 1967, the once popular beach having become largely marsh. (N.F.Gurley)

39. *Merddin Emrys* is working an up train while *Mary Ann* waits with coaches 23 and 12, the latter acting as a static buffet. Also included are *Mountaineer, Upnor Castle, Britomart* and *Linda.* The long shed had been used as a running shed since the railway's revival but its condition continued to deteriorate, necessitating its demolition early in 1988. No. 23 had been repainted in the 1955 livery of green and ivory to mark the Silver Jubilee of the Festiniog Railway Society in 1980. (N.F.Gurley)

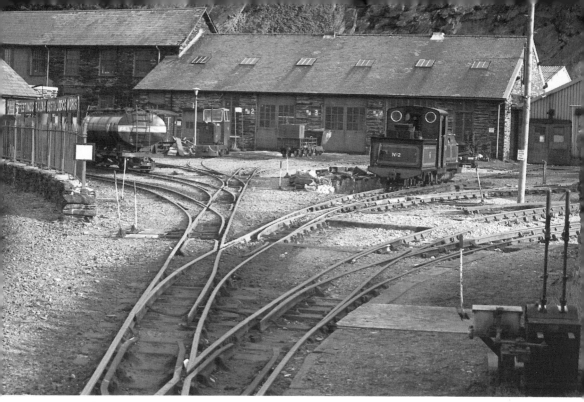

40. The loss of the massive gate pillars, the long shed and the foundry chimney severed links with the past but increased ease of operation. The site of the chimney was used for building an extension which included first floor offices, completed in 1983. No. 2 *Prince* is featured, having been converted to oil firing after being out of use from 1969 until 1980. (N.F.Gurley)

→

42. Seen on 14th February 1994, the old erecting shop retained some overhead shafting but also housed modern machine tools. On the left is the tailstock of a Swift lathe, capable of taking work seven feet long and three feet in diameter. Also visible are six wheels for a new diesel engine, eight for a double engine, a cast iron window frame from the long shed and the firebars and tender of *Palmerston*. (A.Brooks)

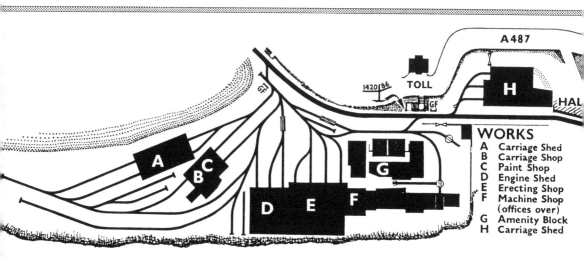

WORKS

A Carriage Shed
B Carriage Shop
C Paint Shop
D Engine Shed
E Erecting Shop
F Machine Shop
   (offices over)
G Amenity Block
H Carriage Shed

41. An unprecedented scene was recorded early on the morning of 1st May 1993, the start of the FR's biennial spectacular steam gala. From left to right, starting at the back, are *Holy War, Irish Mail, Britomart* and *Sgt. Murphy* with *Palmerston* and the 1992 Fairlie *David Lloyd George* in front. Extreme left are *Dolbadarn*, part of *Merddin Emrys, Charles* with *Prince, Linda, Blanche* and the boiler of *Earl of Merioneth*. The steam on the right rises from *Lilla*. Never before have there been so many visiting locomotives. (P.Q.Treloar)

BOSTON LODGE HALT

43. Ground slippage had caused severe track settlement which was rectified by volunteers in the spring of 1955, the new ballast being paid for by the Rev. Timothy Phillips. He had retired to the cottage in the background and appointed himself honorary caretaker of the works, regularly repairing damage from intruders. (R.D.Smith)

44. The locomotive turntable would never be required again and so the caring cleric was allowed to build an unusual garage on it. It had doors at both ends and could be turned to avoid driving in reverse. This and the other turntable (at Glan-y-Pwll) were little used after the 1920s. (A.G.W.Garraway)

45. For the short 1955 season the terminus of the railway was at the north end of the former running shed, seen in pictures 28 and 29. *Prince* worked most trains that year, from August 3rd. After arrival, the empty coaches were propelled back beyond the yard points, uncoupled and connected to a long chain. The engine pulled this while travelling into the yard; the points were changed before the coaches reached them and thus *Prince* returned to the other end of the train. Finally the coaches were propelled up to the halt for the return journey. (A.G.W.Garraway)

46. The platform edging is evident in this December 1983 view of the laying of flat-bottom rail, a type not known on the old FR. The nearest part of the building provided basic accommodation for volunteer workers for many years. (N.F.Gurley)

47. North of the halt, major road improvements in the winter of 1959-60 necessitated provision of a temporary road (right) and level crossing, while the old bridge (centre) was replaced by one of greater road width and railway clearance. The Baldwin diesel *Moelwyn* (so named in 1957) is in attendance although the double Fairlie *Taliesin* hauled most of the spoil for use near Tan-y-bwlch bridge. The new Rhiw Plas bridge opened on 1st June 1960. (N.F.Gurley)

MINFFORDD

48. *Linda* arrives in August 1964, its train including the first coach with raised roof line to enter traffic. This was numbered 14 and had been rebuilt from a Lynton & Barnstaple Railway vehicle in 1963. To the left of this train is the passage leading down to the BR platform. (D.H.Wilson)

49. A steel rope runs from the prefabricated point to *Moel Hebog* which is about to pull it in to place along the two rails on their sides. The points at the other (top) end of the loop had been pulled 90yds by *Moelwyn* on 20th October 1964 to increase the length of the loop. The track on the right and a road parallel to the two large trees lead to Minffordd Yard. The photograph was taken on 28th October 1978. (N.F.Gurley)

50. Minffordd Yard had been laid out in 1872 to facilitate the transfer of goods and mineral traffic between standard and narrow gauge wagons. *Prince* and its reflection are seen on 5th September 1958 when most FR tracks were still hidden by vegetation or debris. (N.F.Gurley)

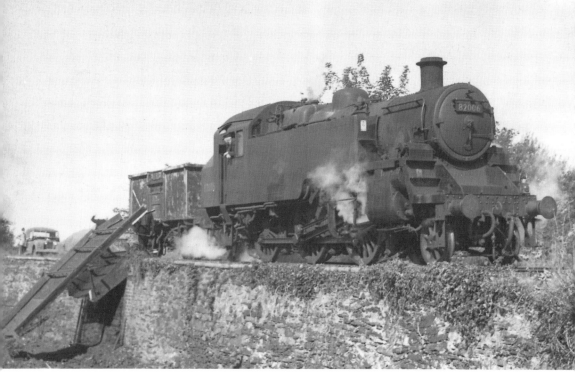

51. Empty ballast wagons rumble down the steep gradient from the main line under gravity, braking being undertaken by members of the London Area Group. Also featured is the former goods transfer shed which, after a period of commercial use as a sawmill, became a workshop for permanent way work. (P.T.Waylett)

52. BR class 3 2-6-2T no. 82006 propels a load of coal for FR locos to the chute. Volunteer workers were often assigned to the filthy and back-breaking task of unloading more than ten tons of coal in high summer. The first part of the chute was fitted with mesh to separate the dirt when ballast was being unloaded. (N.F.Gurley)

53. *Prince* is blasting fiercely as it struggles to raise loaded ballast wagons up the 1 in 30 gradient on the curve from the yard on 17th April 1966. Between the two groups of onlookers is part of the crossover which carried slate wagons, after weighing at Minffordd weigh-house, out onto the main line to Portmadoc Harbour. The historic disc signal was no longer functional. (A.N.Massau)

54. On 17th September 1965, the first day of an Army exercise on the FR, two wagons were derailed on the coal road. The chutes had been re designed to handle the increasing quantities of secondhand BR ballast but the quality of this material became poorer as BR introduced ballast cleaning machinery. New ballast arrived by road after the mid-1970s. (S.Evans)

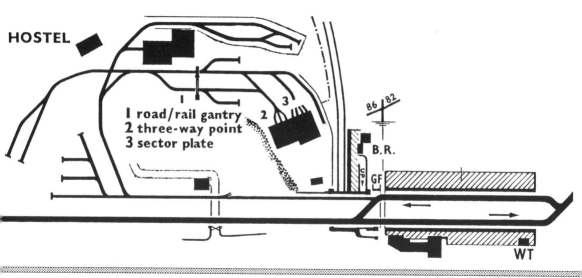

HOSTEL

1 road/rail gantry
2 three-way point
3 sector plate

86 82

B.R.

GF

WT

55. The wharves were still used by a slate merchant in the mid-1960s although all slates had arrived by road for twenty years. The FR train is passing over the BR line, the leading coach being the 1965-built observation car, no. 100. The BR signal box was in use as a ground frame but the timber-clad station of 1872 had been replaced by a simple shelter. (N.F.Gurley)

56. Linda's boiler was despatched to Hunslets on 3rd November 1968 for the fitting of a superheater and a new firebox. JX9002 was the company's third lorry. It was assembled from wartime spares in 1946 as a Leyland Beaver Type 1B and was used for wool transport with a trailer. (N.F.Gurley)

57. Rail stock increased rapidly when over two miles of flat-bottom rail arrived from Tilbury power station on 30th May 1972. Weighing over 150 tons, it was the last major consignment received via BR. A hostel for volunteers was later built to the left of this view. (D.Lusby)

58. A June 1972 photograph includes the former wagon weigh-house, beyond which a line curves right and drops down to the yard, as does the road on the right. The building was converted to an office and store in 1977. The locomotive is Alco 2-6-2T *Mountaineer*, built in the USA in 1917 for use in Europe during World War I. It arrived on the FR on 14th October 1967, having worked most of its life in France. (N.F.Gurley)

59. The impressive dry-stone embankment of Gwyndy Bank runs from Minffordd towards the western part of Penrhyndeudraeth where a halt was established at Pen-y-Bryn. It was a request stop from 1957 until closure in 1967. The 150th anniversary of the opening of the railway was celebrated in April 1986 and among the demonstrations was a slate train hauled by non-FR engines *Chaloner* (left) and *Britomart*. The train is being uncoupled prior to running under gravity through Minffordd station. (N.F.Gurley)

60. This was the state of the track between the station and the level crossing (the gates are on the right) on 27th October 1954, only days before the appearance of the first train in over eight years. (CEA)

61. Two points were removed from the line near Minffordd weigh-house on 1st September 1956 and laid down here to form a loop, as the station was a terminus for the 1957 season. *Taliesin* is about to run round its train, which often carried shoppers to Portmadoc. The hourly service was attractive in that pre-mass motoring age. (FR coll.)

62. The cast-weld joint was introduced on street tramways in the USA in 1894. Horses hauled a mobile cupola along the highway and molten steel was drawn off into a ladle and poured by hand into a mould secured round the previously sand-blasted rail ends. It was more than fifty years before the system was to be regularly used on BR. Here we witness one of the first Thermit welds on a British narrow gauge track on 5th March 1966, this eliminating the problem of fishplate maintenance in the roadway. (N.F.Gurley)

Table 9a   PORTMADOC (Harbour), MINFFORDD and PENRHYNDEUDRAETH—Festiniog

Miles	Up	pm	Saturdays only										
	Portmadoc (H'bour) dep	4 30	..	..	..	..	..	..	..	..	..	..	..
2¼	Minffordd	4 42	..	..	..	..	..	..	..	..	..	..	..
3½	Penrhyndeudraeth	4 50	..	..	..	..	..	..	..	..	..	..	..
7½	Tan-y-Bwlch		Service temporarily suspended				..	..	..	..	..	..	..
9	Dduallt						..	..	..	..	..	..	..
12	Tan-y-Grisiau						..	..	..	..	..	..	..
13¾	Blaenau Ffestiniog arr						..	..	..	..	..	..	..

Miles	Down	pm	Saturdays only			pm					
	Blaenau Ffestiniog dep		Service temporarily suspended				..	..	..	..	..
1¾	Tan-y-Grisiau						..	..	..	..	..
4½	Dduallt						..	..	..	..	..
5½	Tan-y-Bwlch						..	..	..	..	..
9½	Penrhyndeudraeth	1 45	..	..	..	5 0	..	..	..	..	..
11	Minffordd	1 53	..	..	..	5 8	..	..	..	..	..
13¾	Portmadoc (H'bour) arr	2 5	..	..	..	5 20	..	..	..	..	..

All Trains call at Pen Cob, Boston Lodge and Pen-y-Bryn Halts by request

Bradshaw included the one train per week
that was offered to shoppers in the
winter of 1957-58.

63. In order to improve Penrhyn as a passing place for passenger trains, this siding extension had to be provided in May 1969 so that a down trains could enter it and give sufficient clearance at the top points for an up train to pass. Penrhyn had been a crossing place since 1961. There was no train to pass on this dull day in July 1971. (C.Lawson Kerr)

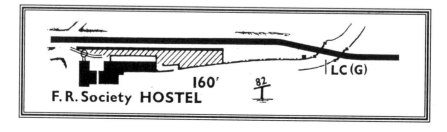

F. R. Society HOSTEL   160'   82   LC (G)

64. The points for a loop at Rhiw Goch were laiid in November 1973 and signalling work started in July 1974. This westward view is from the signal box in August 1975. Trains could then pass regularly here as well as at Dduallt, Tan-y-bwlch and Minffordd. (N.F.Gurley)

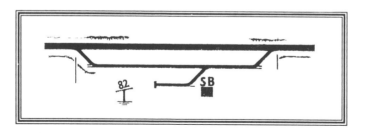

65. The Plas Tan-y-bwlch Estate, including a former quarry owner's mansion, The Plas, was sold in 1962 for development for leisure purposes. High above it, a halt was opened on 1st June 1963 by Mr. John Bibby (left) and the general manager of the FR (centre). The scheme was not developed fully and the property was acquired by Gwynedd County Council for use as a conference and educational centre. (A.G.W.Garraway)

TAN-Y-BWLCH

66. During the closure period the station house continued to be occupied by a former permanent way foreman, who faithfully kept the station points oiled. The vegetation was kept under control by various domestic animals - a rabbit run is evident in this 1954 picture. (CEA)

67. The station was a terminus from 1958 until 1968 and is seen in that first year, before the shortening of the loop in February 1959. Only spot re-sleepering had taken place, the turf coming up to the wheels of *Taliesin* for much of its journey in this vicinity. On the right is the former goods shed, which became a cafe in 1968. (N.F.Gurley)

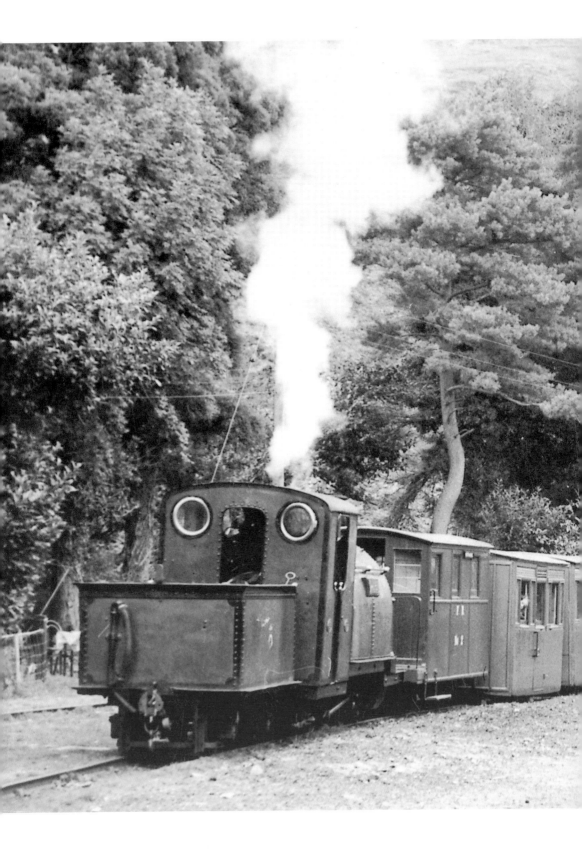

68. In 1958 "The Flying Flea" was assembled at short notice as a relief train owing to overwhelming demand. 4th September 1959 is the date of this photograph. Also recorded is the lorry of R.M.Jones, who supplied all parts of the FR with large quantities of lemonade, orangeade etc, then collectively and commonly known as "far-tade". *Prince* is ready to leave, attached to van no. 2 and some of the original coaches from the mid-1860s. (P.J.Sharpe)

69. Heading *Prince* and assorted coaches is *Merddin Emrys* whose restoration was completed in 1961. It ran devoid of a cab in 1961-2 and as seen here in 1963-66. All available coaches were coupled together at peak times, prior to the introduction of a two-train timetable. (N.F.Gurley)

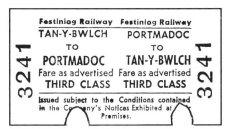

Festiniog Railway   Festiniog Railway
TAN-Y-BWLCH   PORTMADOC
TO   TO
3241   PORTMADOC   TAN-Y-BWLCH   3241
Fare as advertised   Fare as advertised
THIRD CLASS   THIRD CLASS
Issued subject to the Conditions contained in the Company's Notices Exhibited at Premises.

70. *Blanche* runs through with a down works train from the upper part of the line. The refreshment kiosk was in use here from 1965 until 1968, when it was moved to Dduallt. It became known as "The Bunny Hutch" and generated substantial revenue. (N.F.Gurley)

71. An island platform was brought into use on 27th May 1968, just after the introduction of through trains to Dduallt. The 1873 station building (right) was redundant (apart from housing staff instruments) but survived demolition threats to become the subject of a restoration project supported by the Heritage Group in the early 1990s. (N.F.Gurley)

72. An old road tanker body was placed on sleepers and the original tank base to increase capacity, the supply being from the hillside above the station. On the right of this 1971 photograph is the base of a signal box which, although completed, has never functioned as such. Lever interlocking was installed in November 1972 but a change of plan ensued. Automatic crossing of trains became possible here in May 1987 after the provision of point motors and control equipment.
(Festiniog Railway Co.)

73. The cast-iron bridge bears the legend *BOSTON LODGE FOUNDRY 1854*. To relieve the load on this historic structure, reinforced concrete beams were cast inside it, late in 1985. The new *Earl of Merioneth* was recorded in July 1979, taking part in deflection tests. (N.F.Gurley)

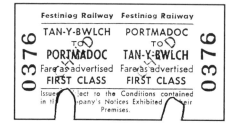

74. Fencing was provided in November 1969 and the footbridge was completed during the following winter, giving access not only to the platform, but also maintaining the right of way to the footpath above the station. Track relaying took place in 1976 and in 1985.
(N.F.Gurley)

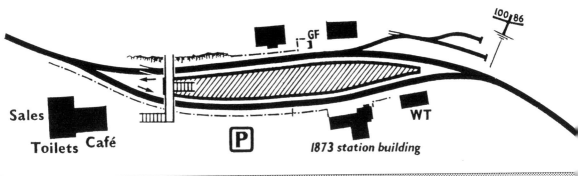

Sales
Toilets Café
P
1873 station building
GF
WT
100 86

75. The footbridge provided a perfect location to record a gravity slate train on 6th June 1993. A train of historic stock waits to return spectators to Porthmadog. The wagons ran from Dduallt to Minffordd, almost the longest run now possible because of the adverse gradient at Tanygrisiau since reopening. (P.H.Abell)

76. After the rebuilding of Rhiw Plas bridge (picture no. 47), the 60yd long Garnedd Tunnel became the most restricting structure on the route. Its clearance with the high profile coach no. 14 is being tested in 1964 in the company of nos. 11 and 12, *Linda* being in charge. (N.F.Gurley)

CAMPBELL'S PLATFORM

DDUALLT

77. *Left* - By the time that this photograph was taken in July 1967, track replacement on the route to Dduallt was well advanced. *Mary Ann* waits for rail to be unloaded, the light-coloured locomotive in the background being privately owned by Colonel Campbell, occupant of Dduallt Manor (right). Beyond the curve on the left the wall deviates to accommodate the old locomotive water tank that was used before line closure. (S.Evans)

78. *Left lower* - Col. Campbell had his own platform and siding. Eventually an aerial ropeway was added for conveyance of goods to the 15th century manor house, as there was no road access to it. Such facilities were unique on the line and so was his contribution to the construction of the Deviation, since he was a licensed handler of explosives. (N.F.Gurley)

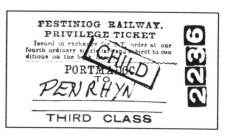

FESTINIOG RAILWAY.
PRIVILEGE TICKET
Issued in exchange for P.T. order at one fourth ordinary single fare and subject to conditions on the back

CHILD

PORTMADOC
TO
PENRHYN

THIRD CLASS

2236

79. *Below* - Drooping rails, rotting sleepers and turf "ballast" were typical form on the upper half of the railway when the single siding at Dduallt was recorded in 1960. This desolate location is far from habitation and must have seen few passengers under the original management, although there had once been a few cottages in the vicinity. It served as a terminus from 1968 to 1977. (I.R.Hunt)

80. The deviation that was constructed to avoid the lake involved building a spiral route to gain height, this part being done entirely by volunteers using pick and shovel, aided by some explosives. Dduallt station is close to the house on the right, the old route running into

the trees at the bottom of the left page. Part of the new embankments can be seen on both pages, the site of the bridge being on the ex-treme right. The nuclear power station at Trawsfynydd dominates the sky-line. (N.F.Gurley)

81. Work is in progress near the trees in the centre of the right page of the previous view on 30th March 1968. The original siding, seen in picture no. 79, was close to the trees and the bridge would be built to the left of this picture. The wagons nearest the camera were side-tippers mounted across another frame to make them suitable for tipping at the end of an embankment. (D.H.Wilson)

82. An open day for local government representatives was held on 7th July 1973, all new-profile coaches being used plus two older ones. *Merddin Emrys* hauled the visitors round the spiral and over the new bridge to the "head of steel". A temporary platform of sleepers was laid and steps were provided down to the picnic tables. It was yet another successful FR special event. (N.F.Gurley)

83. On Bank Holiday Monday 26th May 1975 a shuttle service commenced from Dduallt towards the new tunnel, for visitors to view the new works. This was the first example of push-pull working on the FR. This is the first train and can be seen with the 1836 line on the right and the deviationists' mess on the left. To the left of this is the mouth of the 1842 tunnel. (N.F.Gurley)

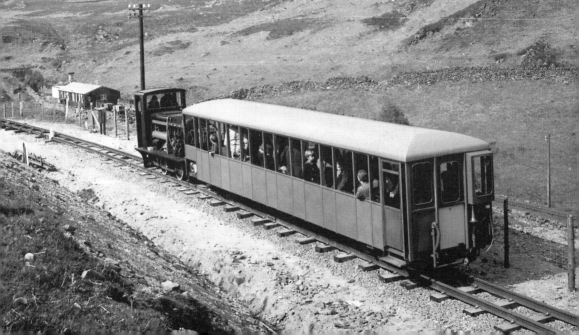

84. Wild goats would sometimes visit the line before it reopened, these being recorded in June 1977 on the old route. These shy creatures now usually remain on higher pastures. (N.F.Gurley)

85. Nearest is *Blanche* with an up train in the summer of 1981, while *Linda* waits by the other water tower. The top loop points were moved to Blaenau Ffestiniog in November 1989 for use on a siding, since which time it has not been possible to pass passenger trains here. Great amounts of rock had had to be removed to make sufficient space for the loop without destroying the mature trees. (N.F.Gurley)

86. The columns and crossbeams of Rhoslyn bridge were erected in January 1969 and formed part of the first spiral railway in Britain. Behind *Linda* is one of two semi-open tourist coaches built by the FR in 1971 on frames of Hudson wagons. Mechanical signalling at this end of the station was commissioned in August 1972 and at the other end in the following April. (N.F.Gurley)

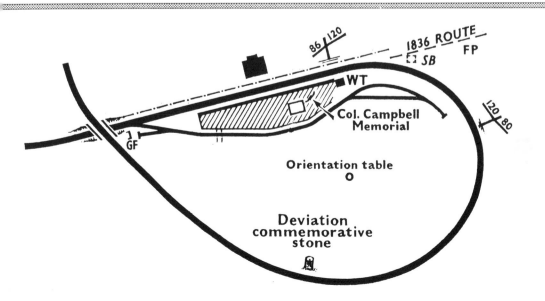

MOELWYN TUNNEL

87. *Prince* took a special train to the south end of the old tunnel on 1st May 1960. The mess seen in picture no. 83 was built later on this widened formation where horses were changed in pre-steam days. The rails at the south end of the tunnel were lifted in 1962, the others between the tunnel and Tanygrisiau having been removed in March 1957. (D.Ferreira)

88. The cutting at the south end of the proposed new tunnel was well advanced when
photographed on 4th June 1975. Tunnelling
commenced on 1st September that year and
breakthrough was achieved on 1st May following, despite a two-week delay resulting from
the collapse of part of this cutting, caused by
heavy rain in February. (R.W.Miller)

89. Stone-screening equipment (right) was set up on the flat area of ground seen in the background of the previous picture. This illustration from 5th October 1975 shows rock from the tunnel arriving on the left and being elevated to the screens where dust, ballast and rock are separated into wagons on three different sidings. Large rocks had to be broken with sledgehammers before being elevated. (N.F.Gurley)

90. After the breakthrough there was much opening out to do, rock bolts to be inserted and drainage to undertake. The entire 287yd long tunnel was shotcreted (sprayed with concrete), the subsequent floor cleaning being very tedious. This is the first steam locomotive through the new tunnel. Aptly, *Mountaineer* propelled a gauging rig through on 28th May 1977 and also observation car no. 100. (N.F.Gurley)

91. The construction of Llyn Ystradau was opposed by the FR but the lake eventually came to enhance the scenery, despite a rise and fall of 18ft depending on electricity demand. Two of the company's lorries deliver rail in the spring of 1976, in readiness for track laying and construction of a loop. (N.F.Gurley)

92. The loop enabled locomotives to run round their trains while the location served as a temporary terminus from 25th June 1977 to 24th June 1978. This is the official opening train, described in caption no. 21. Note that old bull-head rail was used for the short-lived loop. (N.F.Gurley)

93. Water passes between the lakes by way of four high-pressure pipes which the FR crosses on 2ft thick reinforced concrete bridges. These were visible only briefly during their construction in April 1977. (N.F.Gurley)

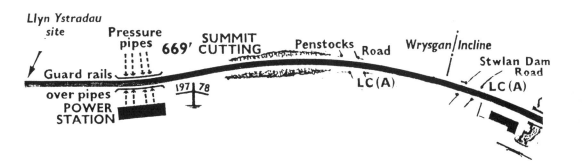

Llyn Ystradau site

Pressure pipes **669'** SUMMIT CUTTING

Penstocks Road

Wrysgan/Incline

Stwlan Dam Road

Guard rails

LC(A)

LC(A)

over pipes **197 78**
POWER STATION

94. This 1980 photograph features the partially submerged formation of the old route. The power station is on the right but the upper lake (Llyn Stwlan) is out of sight up the slope, left of centre; there is a water level difference of about 1000ft. (A.Ll.Lambert)

96. As well as passing behind the power station, the line runs behind this cottage, in front of which the old route was situated (see pictures 105 and 106 in *Branch Lines around Port-*

95. Oil-fired *Prince* is making an unusual amount of smoke as it works a down train at Easter 1983. As the quickest way between Porthmadog and London was (and is) via the FR, the Red Star parcel service was extended to the FR from 9th June 1982. The top of the dam in the background was one of the routes considered for the deviation. (N.F.Gurley)

madoc 1923-46). Blanche is seen in March 1979, approaching the end of its journey at Tanygrisiau. (N.F.Gurley)

97. The rear coach of the 13.30 from Porthmadog on 28th August 1979 is almost on the Stwlan Dam Road crossing while the locomotive is approaching the new Afon Cwmorthin bridge, behind which can be seen the spectacular falls. In the foreground is the Information Centre for those visiting the dam and power station. (P.Q.Treloar)

TANYGRISIAU

98. This was the scene of dereliction in October 1954. The railway north of the tunnel was often used during the closure period by local residents pushing wagons bearing heavy commodities such as coal. Like supermarket trolleys, they were abandoned when empty. (CEA)

99. The abutments for the bridge over the Afon Cwmorthin were constructed at Easter 1976 and, on 27th July following, three telescopic articulated vehicles arrived with the 55ft long beams. A 100-ton crane was hired for positioning them and the concrete decking was poured on site. (N.F.Gurley)

100. The new loop was much longer and at a higher level than its predecessor and is seen nearing completion early in 1978. Left of centre is the old goods shed seen on the left of picture 98. The increase in height of the track can be assessed. (Festiniog Railway Co.)

101. The station was a terminus from 1978 until 1982 and a bus connection was usually available to and from Blaenau Ffestiniog. Here we witness *Blanche* on the opening day, 24th June 1978, the full public service commencing the next day. The locomotive is approaching the Deviationists' train; the other one was the official first train. (N.F.Gurley)

102. Weather conditions on 25th April 1982 were not ideal for the completion of track laying in readiness for the planned reopening in May. Rails and sleepers are carried behind *Blanche*, whose crew would appreciate the tender cab on the return journey. (N.F.Gurley)

103. The loop here was removed in May 1984 but its replacement was anticipated by the construction of a signal box and pointwork in 1993. Steel roller window shutters have been fitted at this vandal-prone location.
(A.Ll.Lambert)

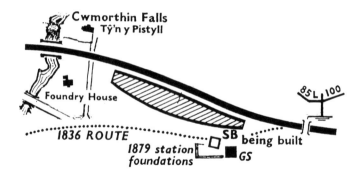

Cwmorthin Falls
Tŷ'n y Pistyll
Foundry House
1836 ROUTE
1879 station foundations
SB being built
GS
85L 100

104. A few weeks later *Blanche* approaches the station and passes over Dolrhedyn bridge, which had been rebuilt on a higher level by the County Council. The capacious chapel has subsequently been demolished. There was a rock fall below the shelf carrying the line in this vicinity, necessitating expensive stabilising measures prior to re-opening. (N.F.Gurley)

105. The Simplex tractor reached Glan-y-Pwll on 31st January 1955 but progress was barred by a fallen wall and tarmac on the level crossing. It was to be 5th March of that year before the former GWR station was reached. The train was then composed of Simplex, coach no. 17 and van no. 1. (A.G.W.Garraway)

106. The roof between the men in the previous picture is on the right of this 1973 view from Oakeley Quarry, then recently closed. Curving in the foreground is the trackbed of the 1899 route to the FR terminus at Dinas. Left of centre is the BR terminus (ex-LMS), with a single track beyond winding under the road bridge towards Trawsfynydd. Some sidings remain on the left, although the narrow gauge ones had long gone. (A.G.W.Garraway)

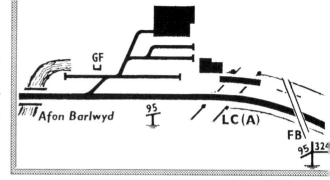

107. The rails on Glan-y-Pwll level crossing were lifted in 1957 and were relaid in 1981, an additional track being added here for possible future use towards the quarry tourist centres. The cottages on the right are FR property and behind them a civil engineering and permanent way depot was established on the site of the old engine shed. *Blanche* draws forward on 22nd March 1982 to run alongside the first BR train to enter the new station. Automatic crossing equipment arrived in 1983. (N.F.Gurley)

108. The house by the level crossing served to accommodate volunteers working on the total relaying of the top end of the railway. *Prince* is returning with a down train on 29th August 1982 and passing the then minimal trackwork of the depot. A new bridge over the Afon Barlwyd (curving from the left) was finished on 1st August 1981. (N.F.Gurley)

BLAENAU FFESTINIOG

109. Here are the ends of some of the standard gauge sidings seen in picture 106, but 21 years earlier when slate was still being transhipped. Other earlier views of these extensive sidings can be seen in pictures 112 to 114 in *Branch Lines around Portmadoc 1923-46.*
(A.G.W.Garraway)

110. The Simplex was recorded at the former exchange platform for the LMS on 15th March 1956 on one of several trips to recover FR slate wagons, many of which were sold for scrap. The footbridge in the background was replaced by a road embankment in 1963 and the platform shelter was sold to a local football club to form part of a stand in Manod.
(A.G.W.Garraway)

111. An April 1961 picture of the former GWR yard features that part of the FR which remained in use until 3rd November 1962. Passenger services to Bala were withdrawn on 4th January 1960 but freight continued until 28th January 1961. The station was "Blaenau Ffestiniog Central" from 18th June 1951. The line to Trawsfynydd was reopened in April 1964 to carry nuclear flask traffic but this involved providing a connection between the two former BR termini at Blaenau Ffestiniog over the FR track-bed. See picture no. 1 for a 1951 view of this location. (P.T.Waylett)

112. This picture from late 1962 is in the opposite direction to the last one. The new road to bypass Tanygrisiau required a bridge which was designed to cross over the new BR connection and the FR branch (right) into the ex-LMS yard. The line on the right as far as the second points had been the FR main line.
(N.F.Gurley)

113. The 1963 bridge (right) had two spans, but the right-hand one which was provided for the narrow gauge track never saw any trains, since slate traffic ceased as the bridge was being built. As part of a bypass scheme for Blaenau, new bridges for the revived FR and proposed Dinas branch were provided. These were built using pre-stressed concrete box sections, which were delivered to the site on 9th June 1980. (N.F.Gurley)

114. New BR track was laid on the route of the former FR main line and a new joint station built on the site of the former Central station. This footbridge to the FR platform was finished in June 1981. The BR loop and platform edge are also complete, their passenger trains using this station from 22nd March 1982. (N.F.Gurley)

115. Heavy snow in December 1981 delayed track laying but *Blanche* reached Glan-y-Pwll with ballast on the 11th. This is the westward panorama in January 1982 as two BR class 25s are sandwiched between the two Crewe snowploughs and FR track work proceeds with difficulty. (N.F.Gurley)

116. The buildings on the left and the white-painted Queen's Hotel also appear in picture no. 111 and help to locate this record of the finished trackwork and platforms. The BR building was tastefully constructed with yellow brick quoins and granite chip infill. The base of the FR water tank (right) was similarly finished. (N.F.Gurley)

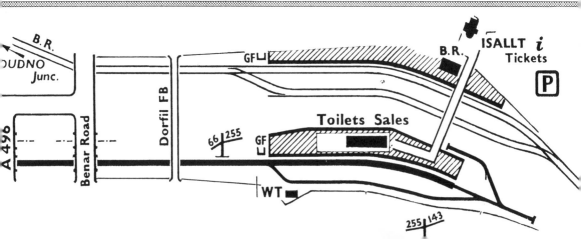

117. The bunting is out on 22nd March 1982 in connection with the opening of the BR platform that day. A "Festiniog Link" headboard was carried by the DMU, which had to wait in the loop for nuclear waste flasks to pass. (The smoke is from the guard's stove). *Blanche* was the first steam engine to reach this location; the wagon was carrying the buffer stops to go at the end of the line. (N.F.Gurley)

118. Regular FR services recommenced on 25th May 1982, after an interval of nearly 43 years. "Service temporarily suspended" on timetables was a statement for political purposes to confirm the intent to reopen. A considerable number of special trains have been run by BR to connect with the FR, this one being recorded on 6th June 1982 while *Merddin Emrys* waits with the connection. (N.F.Gurley)

119. By the time that Planet diesel *Conway Castle* was photographed, running round its train in June 1989, a number of temporary buildings had been erected. The nearest is the "Bunny Hutch", which had earlier served at Tan-y-bwlch and Dduallt. From the reopen- ing, the booking office and tourist information centre were situated in *Isallt*, a Victorian house above the station. One of its chimneys is seen against the sky in the next picture. The shelter was from Acton Main Line station and the toilets came from Tanygrisiau. (N.F.Gurley)

120. A new steel canopy was fabricated and permanent buildings were erected in 1989-90. Space was left on the far side of the platform for an additional track. Thus the over-optimistic vision of a few unusual people some 40 years earlier had reached an unimagined conclusion. Their determination not to allow the most innovative and important narrow gauge railway in the world to pass into oblivion had been justified, despite the sceptics. (N.F.Gurley)

MP Middleton Press

Easebourne Lane, Midhurst, West Sussex. GU29 9AZ
Tel: (0730) 813169 Fax: (0730) 812601

● **Other narrow gauge albums in the same series** ●
by Vic Mitchell and Keith Smith

BRANCH LINE TO SOUTHWOLD

*Britains premier 3ft gauge railway. The elegant locomotives ambled to the
Suffolk coast for 50 years hauling quaint Chinese coaches.
This album provides a lasting visual record.*

BRANCH LINE TO LYNTON

*Devon's much lamented 2ft gauge line. This publication takes readers
on an armchair journey from Barnstaple through tranquil Exmoor to Lynton,
a trip last possible in reality in 1935.*

BRANCH LINES AROUND PORTMADOC 1923-46

*A visual record of the Welsh Highland and Festiniog Railways
during their unsuccessful fight for survival.*

● **Other albums on Colonel Stephens' railways** ●
by Vic Mitchell and Keith Smith

BRANCH LINE TO SELSEY

The West Sussex Railway

BRANCH LINE TO SHREWSBURY

The Shropshire and Montgomeryshire Railway

BRANCH LINE TO TENTERDEN

The Kent & East Sussex Railway

EAST KENT LIGHT RAILWAY

A colliery line that also served local farmers

● **Another book featuring the FR .....** ●

GARRAWAY FATHER AND SON

*Author Allan Garraway was the general manager of the FR for 31 years and
so much of these fascinating biographies relates to the recent story of the line.*

Write or telephone for our full range of over 100 transport books.